On the cover:

The **California mule deer**, also known as "mulies" get their name from their big, mule-like ears. When running, these deer can bounce as if their legs are on springs. They can bounce over a tall fence or bound down a hill with ease. They can move fast too, up to 30 miles per hour!

California Treasures

A Reading/Language Arts Program

Program Authors

Diane August
Donald R. Bear
Janice A. Dole
Jana Echevarria
Douglas Fisher
David Francis
Vicki Gibson
Jan E. Hasbrouck
Scott G. Paris
Timothy Shanahan
Josefina V. Tinajero

 Macmillan/McGraw-Hill

Contributors

Time Magazine, Accelerated Reader

learning through listening

Students with print disabilities may be eligible to obtain an accessible, audio version of the pupil edition of this textbook. Please call Recording for the Blind & Dyslexic at 1-800-221-4792 for complete information.

B

The McGraw·Hill Companies

 Macmillan/McGraw-Hill

Published by Macmillan/McGraw-Hill, of McGraw-Hill Education, a division of The McGraw-Hill Companies, Inc., Two Penn Plaza, New York, New York 10121.

Printed in the United States of America

ISBN: 978-0-02-199961-3/1, Bk. 1
MHID: 0-02-199961-9/1, Bk. 1
6 7 8 9 (RJE/LEH) 12 11

Welcome to
California *Treasures*

Imagine having a pet dinosaur who wants to go to school, learning about how *real* animals act as teams, or reading about a kitten who thinks the moon is a bowl of milk. Your **Student Book** contains these and other award-winning fiction and nonfiction selections.

Treasures Meets California Standards

The instruction provided with each reading selection in your **Student Book** will ensure that you meet all the **California Reading/Language Arts Standards** for your grade. Throughout the book, special symbols (such as ✔) and codes (such as **R 1.1.2**) have been added to show where and how these standards are being met. They will help you know *what* you are learning and *why*.

What do these symbols mean?

CA = Tested Standards in California

✔ = Skill or Strategy that will appear on your test

R = Reading Standards

W = Writing Standards

LC = Language Conventions Standards

LAS = Listening and Speaking Standards

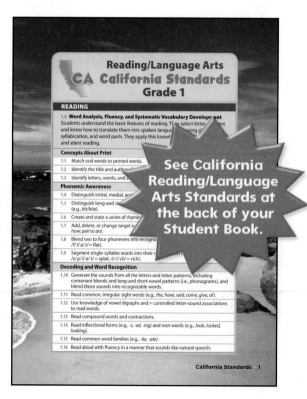

Reading/Language Arts
CA California Standards
Grade 1

READING

1.0 Word Analysis, Fluency, and Systematic Vocabulary Development
Students understand the basic features of reading. They select letter patterns and know how to translate them into spoken language using phonics, syllabication, and word parts. They apply this knowledge and silent reading.

Concepts About Print
1.1 Match oral words to printed words.
1.2 Identify the title and author.
1.3 Identify letters, words, and sentences.

Phonemic Awareness
1.4 Distinguish initial, medial, and final sounds.
1.5 Distinguish long- and short-vowel sounds (e.g., bit/bite).
1.6 Create and state a series of rhyming words.
1.7 Add, delete, or change target sounds (e.g., how; pan to an).
1.8 Blend two to four phonemes into recognizable words. /f/ /l/ /a/ /t/ = flat).
1.9 Segment single-syllable words into their components /s/ /p/ /l/ /a/ /t/ = splat; /r/ /i/ /ch/ = rich).

Decoding and Word Recognition
1.10 Generate the sounds from all the letters and letter patterns, including consonant blends and long- and short-vowel patterns (i.e., phonograms), and blend those sounds into recognizable words.
1.11 Read common, irregular sight words (e.g., the, have, said, come, give, of).
1.12 Use knowledge of vowel digraphs and r-controlled letter-sound associations to read words.
1.13 Read compound words and contractions.
1.14 Read inflectional forms (e.g., -s, -ed, -ing) and root words (e.g., look, looked, looking).
1.15 Read common word families (e.g., -ite, -ate).
1.16 Read aloud with fluency in a manner that sounds like natural speech.

California Standards 1

See California Reading/Language Arts Standards at the back of your Student Book.

McGraw Hill Macmillan/McGraw-Hill

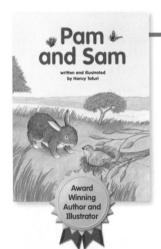

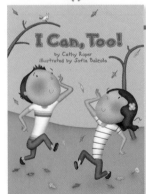

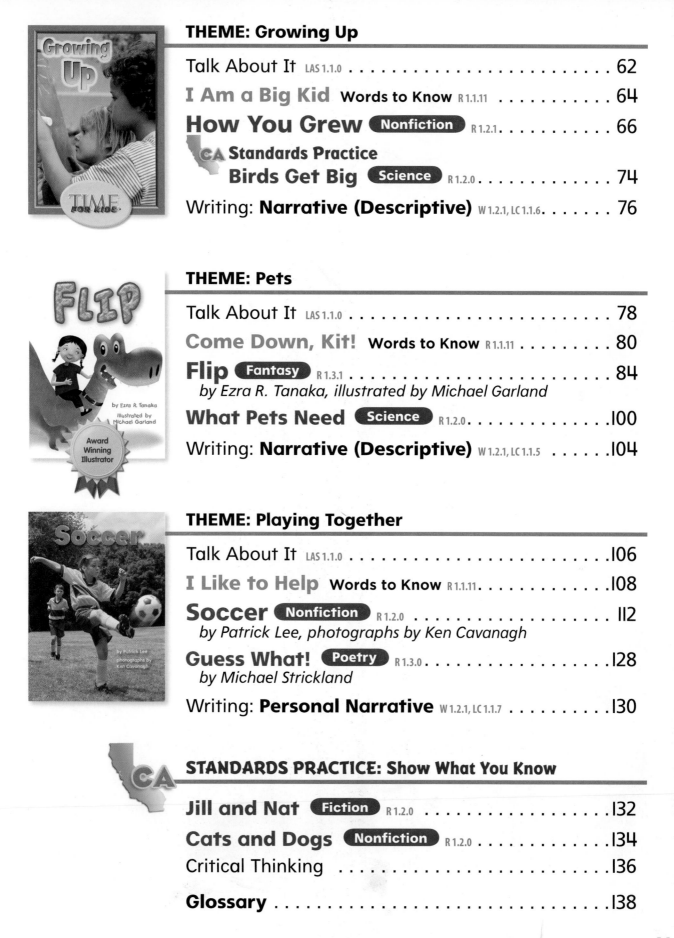

The **Big** Question

What makes you special?

Theme
Launcher
Video

 LOG ON ▶ Find out more about being yourself at **www.macmillanmh.com**.

3

The Big Question

What makes you special?

We are all special! The things we like make us special. So do the games we play, the books we read, and the pictures we draw. Our friends, our families, and even our pets all help to make us one-of-a-kind. What makes you special?

Research Activities

Make an "All About Me" book. You can draw your family and friends and your favorite things. You can even include your name and address, your age, and other facts about you.

Keep Track of Ideas

As you read, keep track of all of the things that make you special. Use the Accordion organizer to draw and write on. Think about your favorite games, books, animals, sports, colors, and places.

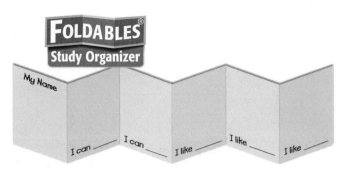

Research Toolkit

Conduct Your Unit 1 Research Online with:

Research Roadmap
Follow step-by-step guide to complete your research project.

Online Resources
- Topic Finder and other Research Tools
- Videos and Virtual Fieldtrips
- Photos and Drawings for Presentations
- Related Articles and Web Resources

California Web Site Links
 Go to **www.macmillanmh.com** for more information.

California People

Maxine Hong Kingston, Writer

Maxine Hong Kingston is a writer. Her mother told her stories about their family in China. Maxine turned those stories into her books.

We Are Special

Talk About It

What do you like to do? What makes you special?

LOG ON ▶ Find out more about being yourself at www.macmillanmh.com.

Nat Can Jump!

Pat can **jump up**.

Nat can **not** jump up.

Nat can jump up!

CA Comprehension

Genre

A **Fantasy** is a made-up story that could not really happen.

Story Structure

Character

Use your Character Chart.

Pam Can	Sam Can

Read to Find Out

What makes Pam and Sam special?

Pam and Sam

written and illustrated
by Nancy Tafuri

Award Winning Author and Illustrator

Pam and Sam play.

Pam ran **up**.

Sam ran up.

Pam and Sam ran.

Pam can **jump**.

Sam can **not** jump.

Sam can not go with Pam.

Look at Sam!

fly

Sam can fly!

Pam and Sam can play.

Say Hello to Nancy Tafuri

Nancy Tafuri says, "I live in the country and love telling stories about animals. I especially like to tell stories about good friends like Pam and Sam. I have fun drawing pictures to go with my stories."

Other books by Nancy Tafuri

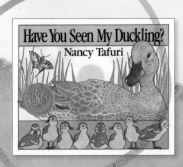

LOG ON ▶ Find out more about Nancy Tafuri at **www.macmillanmh.com**.

CA Author's Purpose

Nancy Tafuri wanted to tell a story about friends. Draw a picture of your friend. Write your friend's name.

CA Critical Thinking

Retell the Story

Use the Retelling Cards
to retell the story in order.

Retelling Cards

Think and Compare

Pam Can	Sam Can
Jump	fly

1. What can Pam do?
   What can Sam do?

2. How are Sam and
   Pam like animals you have seen?

3. How do you know Pam and Sam
   are good friends?

4. How are Sam and Nat in
   "Nat Can Jump!" alike?

Our Best Days

History/Social Science

Genre
Nonfiction tells about real people and things.

Text Feature
Photographs give more information about the text.

Content Vocabulary
neighbor
family
friends

LOG ON Find out more about what kids like at www.macmillanmh.com.

What day is the best day?

26

I like Monday.
I ride my horse.

I like Tuesday.
My **neighbor** and I play.

I like Wednesday.
My **family** has pizza.

I like Thursday.
I help my mom plant.

My **friends** and I like Friday.
What is your best day?

CA **Critical Thinking**

What might Pam and Sam do on their best day?

Write What You Like to Do

Jen wrote a sentence about painting.

I like to paint.

Your Turn

We can do many things.

What can you do?

Write about something you can do.

Writer's Checklist

☑ Did I tell what I like to do?

☑ Does my **sentence** tell a complete thought?

☑ Does my sentence begin with a capital letter?

Ready, Set, Move!

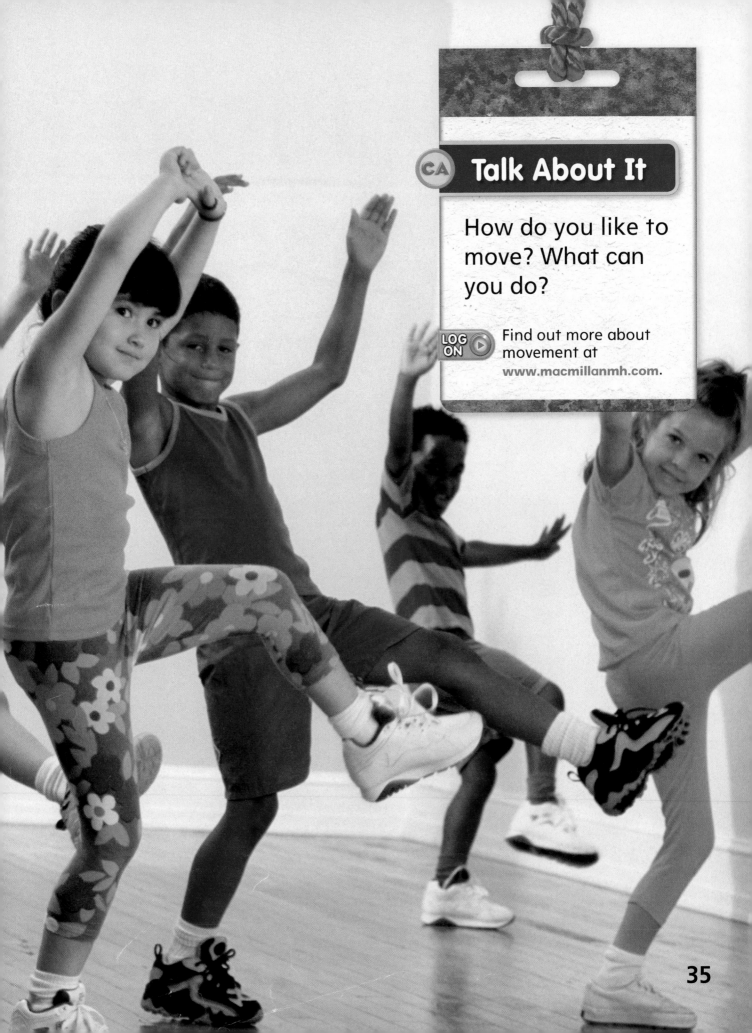

Talk About It

How do you like to move? What can you do?

LOG ON ▶ Find out more about movement at www.macmillanmh.com.

Jump Over It

I can jump **over** **it**.

I can, **too**.

We can not!

 Comprehension

Genre
In a **Rhyming Story**, some words end with the same sound.

Story Structure
Sequence
Use your Sequence Chart.

First

↓

Next

↓

Last

Read to Find Out
What will the girl and boy do together?

40

I Can, Too!

by Cathy Roper

illustrated by Sofia Balzola

Can you do what I can do?

I can! I can do **it, too**.

Can you jump **over** a mat?

Can you jump over a hat?

Can you tag a tree?

Can you tag me?

Can you tap, tap, tap?

I can nap, nap, nap.

Can you do what I can do?

I can! I can, too!

Sofia Balzola Can, Too!

When **Sofia Balzola** was a child, she lived in the mountains. Now she lives by the sea in an old house. She loves to illustrate stories about children doing fun things.

LOG ON ▶ Find out more about Sofia Balzola at www.macmillanmh.com.

CA Illustrator's Purpose

Sofia Balzola likes to draw children doing fun things. Draw yourself having fun. Label your picture.

(CA) Critical Thinking

Retell the Story

Use the Retelling Cards to retell the story.

Retelling Cards

Think and Compare

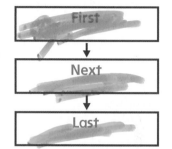

1. What do the children do first? Next? Last?

2. What can the children do that you can do, too?

3. What other fun things can children do together outdoors?

4. How is this story like "Jump Over It"?

Run! Jump! Swim!

CA **Science**

Genre
Nonfiction gives information about a topic.

Text Feature
A Label gives information about a picture.

Content Vocabulary

helps
move
push

LOG ON ▶ Find out more about how animals move at www.macmillanmh.com.

What **helps** animals **move**?

back legs

This kangaroo can jump high.
Strong back legs help it jump.

long legs

This cheetah can run fast.
Long legs help it run.

tail

fins

fins

This shark can swim fast.
Its tail and fins **push** it through
the water.

flipper

flippers

This seal is slow on land.
It is fast in the water.
It swims with wide flippers.

Kids can run, jump, and swim, too. What helps kids move?

 Critical Thinking

Think about *I Can, Too!* How could animals join the fun?

CA **Writing**

✔ **Word Order**

The words in a sentence are in an **order** that makes sense.

Write What You Can Do

Tom wrote a sentence about skating.

I can skate.

Your Turn

Look around the room.

Think about something you can do.

Write about it.

Writer's Checklist

☑ Did I tell what I can do?

☑ Does the order of the words make sense?

☑ Does my sentence end with a special mark?

How have you changed since you were little?

LOG ON ▶ Find out more about growing up at www.macmillanmh.com.

Growing Up

I Am a Big Kid

I am a big kid. What can I do?
I can **run**. I can **ride**.

What can I **be**?
I can be me.

How You Grew

CA Comprehension

Genre
Nonfiction
A nonfiction article gives information about a topic.

Text Structure
Sequence
Look for things babies can do. Look for things kids can do as they get older.

How do kids change as they get older?

Once you were little.

You learned to talk. You could say "mama" and "puppy."

You could sit.
You could dig.

You could eat at the table.
You could sing a song.

You learned to **run** and **ride**.
You could go fast.

How big are you now?
How big will you **be**?

CA Critical Thinking

Tell What You Learned

Describe what kids learn to do as they get bigger.

Think and Compare

1. What can kids learn to do as they grow older?

2. Name some things you learned before you started school.

3. Name two things babies learn that are not in the story.

4. How are the kids in "I Am a Big Kid" different from the kids in "How You Grew"?

CA

Show What You Know

Right There
You can put your finger on the answer.

Birds Get Big

First, a mother bird lays eggs.

Baby birds grow inside.

Then they hatch.

The mother feeds them.

The babies grow big.

Then they fly away.

Go on ▶

CA Standards Practice

Directions: Answer the questions.

1 **What happens first?**

○   ○   ○

2 **What happens after the birds hatch?**

A The birds lay eggs.

B The mother feeds them.

C The birds make a nest.

Tip
Look for
key words.

3 **What happens when the babies are big?**

○   ○   ○

STOP 75

Write About Kids

First Carly drew a picture.
Then she wrote a sentence.

Big kids can ride.

CA Your Writing Prompt

Big kids can do many things.

Now that you are bigger, what can you do?

Write a sentence about it.

Writing Hints

☑ Plan what your sentence will say.

☑ Begin your sentence with a capital letter.

☑ End your sentence with a period.

Pets

CA **Talk About It**

What pets do you know? What are they like?

LOG ON ▶ Find out more about pets at www.macmillanmh.com.

79

Words to Know

come

down

pull

good

Come down,Kit!
Do not **pull** it.

Come to me.

What a **good** cat!

Genre

A **Fantasy** is a made-up story that could not really happen.

Story Structure

Plot

Use your Beginning, Middle, and End Chart.

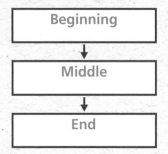

Beginning

↓

Middle

↓

End

Read To Find Out

What will Flip do in school?

84

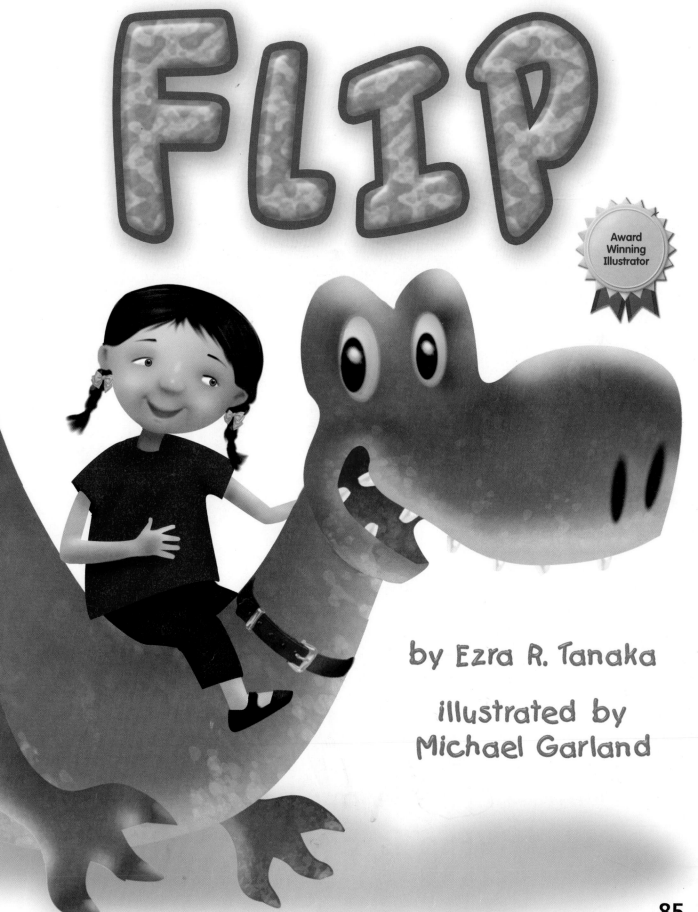

FLIP

Award Winning Illustrator

by Ezra R. Tanaka

illustrated by
Michael Garland

Flip is my pet.
Flip is big.

Flip can not go in.
Flip is sad.

Flip can **pull**!
Flip pulls me in.

Flip and I go to class.

Flip sits.
Be **good**, Flip!

Flip likes class.

The kids like Flip.

Miss Black is mad.
Sit **down**, Flip!

Look at Miss Black!

Flip has a plan.

Look at Flip!
The class claps.

Can Flip **come** back?
"Flip can!" said Miss Black.
Flip is glad!

Meet Michael Garland

When **Michael Garland** was a child, he loved drawing characters from movies and books. Some of his favorite movies and books had funny creatures in them. So he drew a lot of dinousaurs just like Flip!

Other books by Michael Garland

Find out more about Michael Garland at **www.macmillanmh.com**.

CA Illustrator's Purpose

Michael Garland likes to draw dinosaurs. Draw a dinosaur. Label your drawing.

Critical Thinking

Retell the Story

Use the Retelling Cards to retell the story.

Retelling Cards

Think and Compare

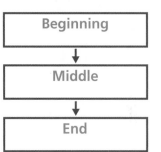

1. What does Flip do in the beginning of the story? What does Flip do when he gets to class?

2. What would you do with Flip if he were your pet?

3. Do you think pets should be allowed in school? Why or why not?

4. How are Flip and Kit in "Come Down, Kit!" alike?

99

What Pets Need

Science

Genre
Nonfiction gives information about a topic.

Text Feature
A List is a series of things written in order.

Content Vocabulary
need
living things
care

LOG ON ▶ Find out more about pets at www.macmillanmh.com.

What do pets **need**?

Like all **living things**, pets need food.
Some pets eat seeds or plants.

Some pets eat meat or fish.
All pets need fresh water.

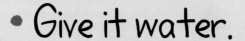

Caring for My Rabbit

- Give it food.
- Give it water.
- Change the bedding.
- Brush the fur.

Pets need a safe home.
Pets need our love and **care**.

 Critical Thinking

How would you take care of Flip?

103

✓ **Exclamation**

An **exclamation** is a sentence that shows strong feeling.

Write About a Pet

Robert wrote about a dog.

Boo is really smart!

Your Turn

Some pets are very special.

Think about a pet you know.

Write to tell why this pet is special.

Writer's Checklist

☑ Will the reader know how I feel?

☑ Does my sentence show strong feelings?

☑ Does my exclamation end with an exclamation mark?

Playing Together

What do you like doing with your friends?

LOG ON ▶ Find out more about playing together at www.macmillanmh.com.

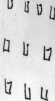

I Like to Help

✔ **Words to Know**

help

now

use

very

I like to **help** Hank.
I help him dig.

Now I **use** my hands.

It looks **very** good!

CA Comprehension

Genre

Nonfiction gives information about a topic.

Text Structure

Author's Purpose
Use your Author's Purpose Chart.

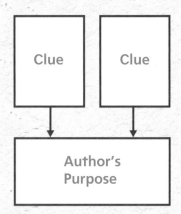

Clue Clue

Author's Purpose

Read to Find Out

Why did the author write *Soccer*?

Soccer

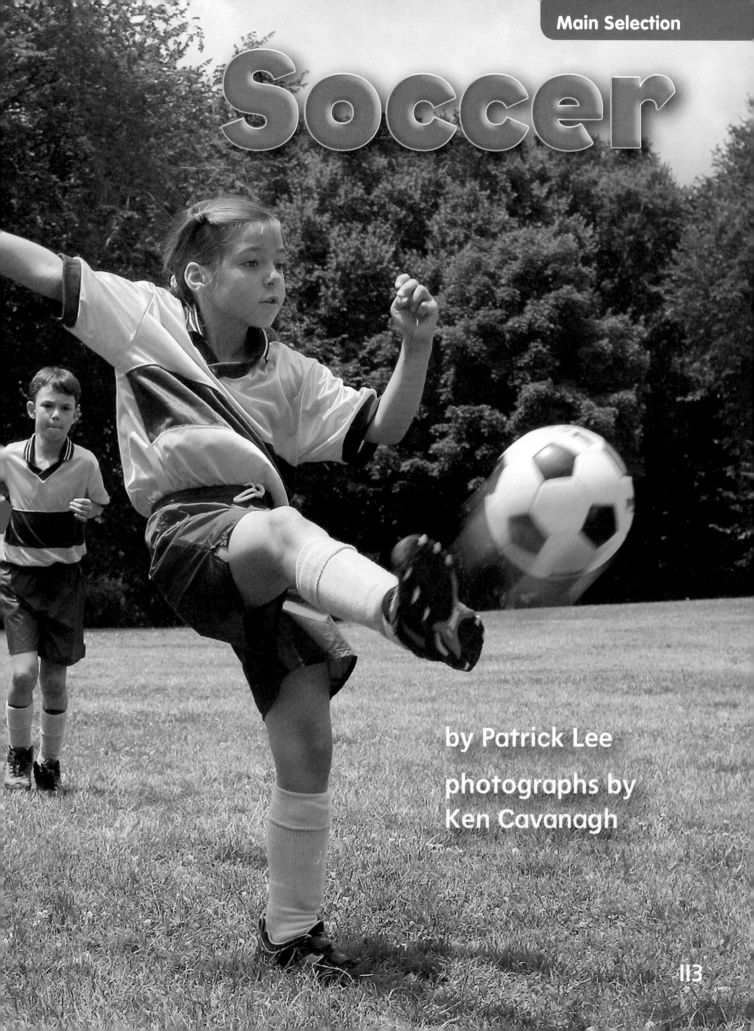

by Patrick Lee

photographs by
Ken Cavanagh

We play soccer.

Hank will **help**.
We like Hank!

We run and kick.

I kick and kick.

I am **very** fast.
I am as fast as the wind!

I can not **use** my hands.

I can kick the ball.
I will pass it to Jill.

I can zig and zag.
I am very fast.

I can use my hands.

Where will the ball land?

It lands here.
I did it!

Now it is over.
We like soccer!

Meet the Photographer

Ken Cavanagh says, "Many photographers like to take pictures of one or two things, like sports or family events. I enjoy taking pictures of many things. Besides sports, I like to take pictures of people, places, and nature."

LOG ON Find out more about Ken Cavanagh at **www.macmillanmh.com**.

CA Photographer's Purpose

Ken Cavanagh wanted to show how soccer is played. Draw someone playing a sport. Label the picture.

Critical Thinking

Retell the Selection

Use the Retelling Cards to retell the selection in order.

Retelling Cards

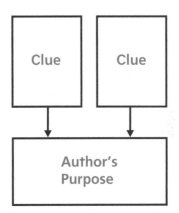

Think and Compare

1. What did the author want you to learn from the selection?

2. What games do you like to play? Why do you like them?

3. How do soccer players work as a team?

4. How is the soccer team like the girl and Hank in "I Like to Help"?

Poetry

Genre
In a Poem, words often rhyme.

✔ **Literary Element**
Words that rhyme end with the same sound.

LOG ON ▶ Find out more about playing together at www.macmillanmh.com.

READ TOGETHER

Guess What!

by Michael R. Strickland

Black and white
Kicked with might

Smooth and round
Air bound

Passed and rolled
Toward the goal

Rise and fall
A soccer ball.

CA **Critical Thinking**

What do both *Soccer* and "Guess What!"
tell about how to play soccer?

✔ **Writing Sentences**

A **sentence** begins with a capital letter and ends with a special mark.

Write About Playing Together

Pat wrote about building with blocks.

Ray and I play with blocks.

We make big towns.

Your Turn

Think of something you play with your friends. Draw a picture. Write about it.

Writer's Checklist

☑ Did I tell what my friend and I like to do?

☑ Does each **sentence** tell a complete thought?

☑ Does each sentence begin with a capital letter?

Review

Character
Setting
Sequence
Photographs
Labels

READ TOGETHER
Jill and Nat

Jill is six.

She digs in the sand.

Then she plays with Nat.

Nat is six, too.

He rides up the hill.

Then he rides back down.

READ TOGETHER

Cats and Dogs

A cat can jump.
A cat can go up a tree.

A cat can move its ears.
It can move its whiskers.
It can lick its paws.

Look at the cat on the grass.
The cat goes, "Purr!"

whiskers

paw

ear

A dog can run.
A dog can jump, too.

A dog has a good nose.
A dog can dig and dig.
It can dig with its paws.

Look at the dog wag its tail.
The dog goes, "Woof!"

nose

tail

paw

CA Critical Thinking

Now answer the questions. Base your answers on the story "Jill and Nat."

1 **What does Jill do first?**

A play with Nat

B go to school

C dig in the sand

2 **The setting of the story is in a _____ .**

A park

B house

C school

3 **What do Jill and Nat like to do?**

Write about it.

Now answer the questions. Base your answers on the story "Cats and Dogs."

1 **What is the dog doing in the picture?**

A eating

B standing

C sleeping

2 **What body part on the cat has a label?**

A tail

B leg

C whiskers

Write on Demand

PROMPT What do you know about cats and dogs? Write as much as you can and as well as you can.

Glossary

What Is a Glossary?

A glossary can help you find the meanings of words. The words are listed in alphabetical order. You can look up a word and read it in a sentence. There is a picture to help you.

fly

fast

Sample Entry

Letter

M m

Main Entry

mat

Sentence

I wipe my feet on the **mat**.

pet

Cc

clap

A seal can **clap**.

Dd

dig

We can **dig** in the sand.

Ff

fast

I run **fast**.

fly

Birds **fly** in the sky.

Hh

hat

The boy has a red **hat**.

help

Amy gets **help** from her dad.

Kk

kick

Nan likes to **kick** the ball.

Mm

mat

I wipe my feet on the **mat**.

Nn

nap

Jill takes a **nap**.

Pp

pet

I love my **pet** dog.

pull

I **pull** this wagon.

Rr

---

ride

I go for a **ride** on my bike.

Acknowledgments

The publisher gratefully acknowledges permission to reprint the following copyrighted material:

"Guess What!" by Michael Strickland. Copyright © 2000 by HarperCollins. Reprinted with permission of HarperCollins, NY.

Book Cover, HAVE YOU SEEN MY DUCKLING? by Nancy Tafuri. Copyright © 1996 by Nancy Tafuri. Reprinted by permission of Greenwillow Books.

Book Cover, SPOTS FEATHERS AND CURLY TAILS by Nancy Tafuri. Copyright © 1988 by Nancy Tafuri. Reprinted by permission of Greenwillow Books.

ILLUSTRATIONS
Cover Illustration: Mary Jane Begin

8-11: Tomislav Zlatic. 12–23: Nancy Tafuri. 26–31: Eileen Hine. 32: Diane Paterson. 36–39: Diane Greenseid. 40–53: Sofia Balzola. 80–83: Amanda Haley. 84–99: Michael Garland. 108–111: Elivia Savadier. 114: Jon Nez. 116: Jon Nez. 118–125: Jon Nez. 128–129: Cheryl Mendenhall. 130: Ken Bowser. 132–133: Benton Mahan. 139–140: Carol Koeller. 140–145: Carol Koeller.

PHOTOGRAPHY
All Photographs are by Ken Cavanagh or Ken Karp for Macmillan/McGraw-Hill (MMH) except as noted below.

Inside front & back covers: Royalty-Free/CORBIS. v: Kevin Fitzgerald/Getty Images. 2-3: Jose Luis Pelaez/Getty Images. 3: Westend61/Alamy. 4: Tim Pannell/CORBIS. 5: Doug Menuez/CORBIS. 6-7: Purestock/PunchStock. 24: Courtesy of Nancy Tafuri. 27: Brand X Pictures/Getty Images. 28: Image Source/Alamy. 29: Brand X Pictures/Alamy. 30: SW Productions/Brand X Pictures/Alamy. 31: Tom & Dee Ann McCarthy/CORBIS. 32: Dynamic Graphics Group/Creatas/Alamy. 33: C SQUARED STUDIOS/Getty Images. 34-35: Ariel Skelley/CORBIS. 52: Courtesy of Ana Costales. 54: Mike Hill/AGE Fotostock. 55: Medford Taylor/National Geographic Image Collection. 56: Tom Brakefield/CORBIS. 57: Jeffrey L. Rotman/CORBIS. 58: (tc) David Madison/Getty Images; (br) Peter Scoones/Getty Images. 59: Bob Gomel/CORBIS. 60: Comstock. 61: (t) Ingram Publishing/Alamy; (tr) C Squared Studios/Getty Images. 62-63: Kevin Fitzgerald/Getty Images. 64: (tl) David Stoecklein/CORBIS; (c) Photodisc/Getty Images. 65: Lawrence Migdale/Photo Researchers. 66: Digital Vision/PunchStock. 67: Photodisc/PunchStock. 68: (t) Blaine Harrington/CORBIS; (b) Elyse Lewin/Getty Images. 69: Lawrence Migdale/Photo Researchers. 70: (t) Don Smetzer/Photo Edit; (b) Cheryl Clegg/Index Stock. 71: (tl) Myrleen Ferguson Cate/Photo Edit; (b) David Muscroft/SuperStock. 72: Digital Vision/PunchStock. 74: Darren Bennett/Animals Animals. 75: (tl) Darren Bennett/Animals Animals; (tc) Don Enger/Animals Animals; (tr, bl, bc) MICHAEL HABICHT/Animals Animals; (br) JOE MC DONALD/Animals Animals. 76: Brand X Pictures/Getty Images. 77: (c) Bet Noire/Shutterstock; (b) C Squared Studios/Getty Images. 78-79: Timothy Shonnard/Getty Images. 98: Courtesy of Michael Garland. 100: Gabe Palmer/CORBIS. 101: (t) Richard Hutchings/Photo Edit; (b) Robert Maier/Animals Animals. 102: PhotoStockFile/Alamy. 103: Steve Satushek/Getty Images. 104: Kevin Radford/Masterfile. 105: (tr) Yiap/AGE Fotostock; (t) Bildagentur Franz Waldhaeusl/Alamy. 106-107: Blend Images/Jupiter Images. 130: Jose Luis Pelaez/Getty Images. 134-135: G.K. & Vikki Hart/Getty Images. 138: (cl) Steve Hamblin/Alamy; (br) Norbert Schaefer/CORBIS. 139: (c) Stephen Wisbauer/Jupiter Images; (b) Michael Keller/CORBIS. 141: (t) Norbert Schaefer/CORBIS; (b) Steve Hamblin/Alamy. 142: Digital Vision Direct. 143: Stephen Wisbauer/Jupiter Images. 144: Michael Keller/CORBIS. 145: Photodisc Red/Getty Images. CA Standards pages 1-4: Medioimages/PunchStock.

Reading/Language Arts
CA California Standards
Grade 1

READING

1.0 Word Analysis, Fluency, and Systematic Vocabulary Development

Students understand the basic features of reading. They select letter patterns and know how to translate them into spoken language by using phonics, syllabication, and word parts. They apply this knowledge to achieve fluent oral and silent reading.

Concepts About Print

1.1	Match oral words to printed words.
1.2	Identify the title and author of a reading selection.
1.3	Identify letters, words, and sentences.

Phonemic Awareness

1.4	Distinguish initial, medial, and final sounds in single-syllable words.
1.5	Distinguish long-and short-vowel sounds in orally stated single-syllable words (e.g., *bit/bite*).
1.6	Create and state a series of rhyming words, including consonant blends.
1.7	Add, delete, or change target sounds to change words (e.g., change *cow* to *how; pan* to *an*).
1.8	Blend two to four phonemes into recognizable words (e.g., /c/ a/ t/ = cat; /f/ l/ a/ t/ = flat).
1.9	Segment single-syllable words into their components (e.g., /c/ a/ t/ = cat; /s/ p/ l/ a/ t/ = splat; /r/ i/ ch/ = rich).

Decoding and Word Recognition

1.10	Generate the sounds from all the letters and letter patterns, including consonant blends and long-and short-vowel patterns (i.e., phonograms), and blend those sounds into recognizable words.
1.11	Read common, irregular sight words (e.g., *the, have, said, come, give, of*).
1.12	Use knowledge of vowel digraphs and *r-* controlled letter-sound associations to read words.
1.13	Read compound words and contractions.
1.14	Read inflectional forms (e.g., *-s, -ed, -ing*) and root words (e.g., *look, looked, looking*).
1.15	Read common word families (e.g., *-ite, -ate*).
1.16	Read aloud with fluency in a manner that sounds like natural speech.

Vocabulary and Concept Development

1.17 Classify grade-appropriate categories of words (e.g., concrete collections of animals, foods, toys).

2.0 Reading Comprehension

Students read and understand grade-level-appropriate material. They draw upon a variety of comprehension strategies as needed (e.g., generating and responding to essential questions, making predictions, comparing information from several sources). The selections in *Recommended Literature, Kindergarten Through Grade Twelve* illustrate the quality and complexity of the materials to be read by students. In addition to their regular school reading, by grade four, students read one-half million words annually, including a good representation of grade-level-appropriate narrative and expository text (e.g., classic and contemporary literature, magazines, newspapers, online information). In grade one, students begin to make progress toward this goal.

Structural Features of Informational Materials

2.1 Identify text that uses sequence or other logical order.

Comprehension and Analysis of Grade-Level-Appropriate Text

2.2 Respond to *who, what, when, where,* and *how* questions.

2.3 Follow one-step written instructions.

2.4 Use context to resolve ambiguities about word and sentence meanings.

2.5 Confirm predictions about what will happen next in a text by identifying key words (i.e., signpost words).

2.6 Relate prior knowledge to textual information.

2.7 Retell the central ideas of simple expository or narrative passages.

3.0 Literary Response and Analysis Students read and respond to a wide variety of significant works of children's literature. They distinguish between the structural features of the text and the literary terms or elements (e.g., theme, plot, setting, characters). The selections in *Recommended Literature, Kindergarten Through Grade Twelve* illustrate the quality and complexity of the materials to be read by students.

Narrative Analysis of Grade-Level-Appropriate Text

3.1 Identify and describe the elements of plot, setting, and character(s) in a story, as well as the story's beginning, middle, and ending.

3.2 Describe the roles of authors and illustrators and their contributions to print materials.

3.3 Recollect, talk, and write about books read during the school year.

WRITING

1.0 Writing Strategies Students write clear and coherent sentences and paragraphs that develop a central idea. Their writing shows they consider the audience and purpose. Students progress through the stages of the writing process (e.g., prewriting, drafting, revising, editing successive versions).

Organization and Focus

1.1	Select a focus when writing.
1.2	Use descriptive words when writing.

Penmanship

1.3	Print legibly and space letters, words, and sentences appropriately.

2.0 Writing Applications (Genres and Their Characteristics) Students write compositions that describe and explain familiar objects, events, and experiences. Student writing demonstrates a command of standard American English and the drafting, research, and organizational strategies outlined in Writing Standard 1.0.

Using the writing strategies of grade one outlined in Writing Standard 1.0, students:

2.1	Write brief narratives (e.g., fictional, autobiographical) describing an experience.
2.2	Write brief expository descriptions of a real object, person, place, or event, using sensory details.

WRITTEN AND ORAL ENGLISH LANGUAGE CONVENTIONS

The standards for written and oral English language conventions have been placed between those for writing and for listening and speaking because these conventions are essential to both sets of skills.

1.0 Written and Oral English Language Conventions Students write and speak with a command of standard English conventions appropriate to this grade level.

Sentence Structure

1.1	Write and speak in complete, coherent sentences.

Grammar

1.2	Identify and correctly use singular and plural nouns.
1.3	Identify and correctly use contractions (e.g., *isn't, aren't, can't, won't*) and singular possessive pronouns (e.g., *my/ mine, his/ her, hers, your/s*) in writing and speaking.

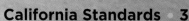

Punctuation

1.4	Distinguish between declarative, exclamatory, and interrogative sentences.
1.5	Use a period, exclamation point, or question mark at the end of sentences.
1.6	Use knowledge of the basic rules of punctuation and capitalization when writing.

Capitalization

1.7	Capitalize the first word of a sentence, names of people, and the pronoun *I*.

Spelling

1.8	Spell three-and four-letter short-vowel words and grade-level-appropriate sight words correctly.

LISTENING AND SPEAKING

1.0 Listening and Speaking Strategies Students listen critically and respond appropriately to oral communication. They speak in a manner that guides the listener to understand important ideas by using proper phrasing, pitch, and modulation.

Comprehension

1.1	Listen attentively.
1.2	Ask questions for clarification and understanding.
1.3	Give, restate, and follow simple two-step directions.

Organization and Delivery of Oral Communication

1.4	Stay on the topic when speaking.
1.5	Use descriptive words when speaking about people, places, things, and events.

2.0 Speaking Applications (Genres and Their Characteristics) Students deliver brief recitations and oral presentations about familiar experiences or interests that are organized around a coherent thesis statement. Student speaking demonstrates a command of standard American English and the organizational and delivery strategies outlined in Listening and Speaking Standard 1.0.

Using the speaking strategies of grade one outlined in Listening and Speaking Standard 1.0, students:

2.1	Recite poems, rhymes, songs, and stories.
2.2	Retell stories using basic story grammar and relating the sequence of story events by answering *who, what, when, where, why,* and *how* questions.
2.3	Relate an important life event or personal experience in a simple sequence.
2.4	Provide descriptions with careful attention to sensory detail.

LuzMaria

72345 678

luzmaria